The Tale of
PALE MALE
A TRUE STORY

JEANETTE WINTER

HARCOURT, INC.

Orlando   Austin   New York   San Diego   Toronto   London

Requests for permission to make copies of any part of the work should be submitted online at
www.harcourt.com/contact or mailed to the following address: Permissions Department,
Harcourt, Inc., 6277 Sea Harbor Drive, Orlando, Florida 32887-6777.

www.HarcourtBooks.com

Library of Congress Cataloging-in-Publication Data
Winter, Jeanette.
The tale of pale male: a true story/Jeanette Winter.
p.   cm.
1. Red-tailed hawk—New York (State)—New York—Anecdotes.   I. Title.
QL696.F32W555   2007
598.9'44—dc22   2006008741
ISBN 978-0-15-205972-9

H G F E D C B

Printed in Singapore

The illustrations in this book were done in acrylic on Arches watercolor paper.
The display type was set in Syntax Black & OptiEagle Bold.
The text type was set in Syntax Bold.
Color separations by Colourscan Co. Pte. Ltd., Singapore
Printed and bound by Tien Wah Press, Singapore
This book was printed on totally chlorine-free Stora Enso Matte paper.
Production supervision by Pascha Gerlinger
Designed by Judythe Sieck

If you look hard out in the world, you might see
the nest of a Red-tailed Hawk
high up on a cliff,
or high up in a tall tree,
or, if there are no trees,
at the very top of a tall cactus.

Hawks like a tall perch
so they can see what is happening down below.
Nothing escapes the eye of a Redtail,
not even a tiny hurrying, scurrying mouse.

This Redtail has just caught a mouse
in the countryside below.

But look—there are skyscrapers all around.
And what building is the Redtail headed for?
It's the Metropolitan Museum of Art.
The Metropolitan Museum is in Central Park.
And Central Park is in New York City.
This Redtail is a city slicker!

A lady hawk waits for the Redtail.
He offers her his gift.
She takes it.
And eats it.

She would rather have a mouse to eat
than anything else.
The hawks become mates,
and soar high into the sky.

The two Redtails break twigs,
just the right length,
to build a nest.

They bring each twig to a window top
guarded by angels—
back and forth, back and forth,
over and over—
until the nest is built.
Spikes for keeping pigeons away
hold the twigs secure.

Below on the ground,
bird-watchers have spotted the two hawks
that they had named Pale Male and Lola.
Look!
They're nesting again
at their penthouse on Fifth Avenue.

Lola settles into their home,
as Pale Male flies back and forth, back and forth,
bringing provisions to the mother-to-be.

Evidence of Lola's meals
falls to the balcony below.
The people living there are *not* happy about it!

As spring blossoms appear on the trees,
Pale Male and Lola
perch on the edge of their nest—
moving up and down, up and down,
dropping food in.
Are baby chicks hidden there?

Yes!
At last the chicks peek out—
all downy soft like dandelions.
And below, the watchers cheer.

Mama and Papa stay busy—
back and forth, back and forth—
bringing food for their two hungry chicks.

When the blossoms give way to leaves,
the fledglings—fuzzy chicks no more—
practice using their wings.
Flit flap, flit flap, flit flap—
they want to fly!

At last the fledglings are ready.
They perch on the edge of the nest
for a long, long time.
And then—flit flap, flit flap—
they lift off into the air.
Will they fall?

No!
The fledglings land safely
on nearby buildings.
Happy watchers applaud.

The young birds fly from ledge to ledge—
the buildings like trees,
the ledges like branches.
Pale Male shows them how to flap and glide.

Soon the fledglings fly over the traffic
on Fifth Avenue to Central Park.
Mama and Papa teach their young birds to hunt.
Mice and rats are tastiest,
but a plump pigeon will do nicely.

The Redtails hunt, glide, soar, and dive all day,
and then at twilight return to their home on high.
By now the hawk family is famous.

But not everyone loves the hawks.
On a cold, rainy day in December—
when no one is watching—
the apartment people install a window-washer platform
near the empty winter nest.

Workers stuff all four hundred pounds
of the carefully gathered sticks, twigs,
and bits of bark into big plastic bags—
even the pigeon spikes that supported the nest.
The apartment people are happy.
No more falling bones. No more mess!

By morning everyone knows what happened.
Newspapers, TV, and radio all tell the story
of the stolen nest on Fifth Avenue.

The next day watchers gather at the building.
Each day more bird lovers come,
until the crowd grows to hundreds.

The apartment people are in a huff about the crowds.
So finally they meet with the watchers
to discuss the situation.

Ah, victory!
The watchers convince the apartment people
to let the hawks build a new nest.
A cheer goes up when the spikes are replaced.

The fledglings have grown up and gone,
but Pale Male and Lola begin gathering twigs
for their new nest—
back and forth, back and forth . . .

because even for Red-tailed Hawks
living atop a tall building,
high above the traffic and crowds
of New York City,
there's no nest
like home.

AUTHOR'S NOTE

Pale Male, a Red-tailed Hawk so named because of his paler-than-usual coloring, was first sighted in New York City in 1991. After a few unsuccessful attempts at building a nest in Central Park, in 1993 he and his mate settled on a perch atop 927 Fifth Avenue, a twelve-story apartment just across the street. This was the first time Red-tailed Hawks had nested in Manhattan, and devoted bird lovers kept track of their every move.

Over the years Pale Male has had several mates—First Love, Chocolate, Blue, and Lola—and since 1995 he has fathered more than twenty chicks.

The removal of the eight-foot-wide nest and the pigeon spikes on December 7, 2004, galvanized bird lovers everywhere, but especially in New York City. The persistence of their protests led to negotiations with the board of the apartment building, which resulted in replacement of the pigeon spikes. Pale Male and Lola returned to build a new nest, and as of spring 2006, the hawks were still in residence there. But even if they move to another building, the hope is that they will continue to raise New York City chicks.